Praise for The Book of Divine Love: Heart Opening Poems

"This exquisite little book is a divine companion for days when we need a reminder that our greatest resource—love— lies within us. We only have to access and experience its life-changing glow. Mary Burnett Brown's poems are an encouraging and uplifting way to do just that."

SOPHFRONIA SCOTT, author of *The Seeker and the Monk: Everyday Conversations with Thomas Merton*

"Reading Mary Burnett Brown is like strolling through an ancient serene cloister. Her meditative prayer/poems could have been written centuries ago or centuries from now, for they spring from a timeless, ageless wisdom. She turns us again and again to "the splendor in the ordinary" and the "deep wells of delight." Drink from this volume whenever your soul thirsts."

IRENE O'GARDEN, Off-Broadway playwright, award winning poet and author of *Glad to Be Human*

"Mary Burnett Brown's poems offer you an opportunity to settle into a heart-based conversation with the divine whisperings of the soul. Her poems, when experienced as a meditation, can be absorbed at a visceral level, providing love and comfort especially during these times of uncertainty in our world."

GLENDA CEDARLEAF, MSW, Guided Imagery Meditation Recording Artist, Heart-Centered Hypnotherapist and author of *A Guide to Writing and Recording Guided Imagery Meditations:70 Healing Scripts Included and Meditative Bedtime Stories*

"Mary's poetry always has an underlying energy of love, light and divine wisdom. The first poem I read of Marys touched my soul in a really beautiful way and many poems later I still feel that beautiful feeling. Her poetry is pure love that can be felt as you read her work. It is a gift she has to share the energy of love, light and divine wisdom in the form of her poetry. Her poems are timeless and encourages you to pause for a moment to embrace the beauty and love in our world."

CARRIE SABA, Your EFT Tapping Coach

The Book

OF

Divine Love

HEART OPENING
POEMS

The Book

OF

Divine Love

HEART OPENING
POEMS

MARY BURNETT BROWN

Heartfelt Poetry LLC
Woodland Park, Colorado

Heartfelt Poetry, LLC
info@heartfeltpoetryllc.com

Ordering Information:
Quantity sales. Special discounts are available on quantity purchases by corporations, associations, and others. Please email the publisher at:
info@heartfeltpoetryllc.com

The Book of Divine Love: Heart Opening Poems/Mary Burnett Brown. —1st ed.

Paperback: ISBN 978-1-7355446-0-1
eBook: ISBN 978-1-7355446-1-8

To my husband, Tom Brown,
whose love and support have encouraged me
to find my happy place.

Contents

FOREWORD

For many years, I thought there was only one poet, Robert Frost.

Maybe it was because I grew up in the 1960s seeing Robert Frost read a poem at President Kennedy's inauguration. Even though I was only five at the time, I could sense his words created emotion and feeling and set the stage for something important, inspiring and transformative.

"Poetry is when an emotion has found its thought and the thought has found words," Frost wrote.

I grew up a lover of words and later a journalist and author, so you can imagine my delight when I eventually discovered there was a world of poets and poetry!

Today you are holding in your hands the work of a more recent favorite poet of mine, Mary Burnett Brown.

Every week for more than a year, I've eagerly awaited the gems written by this international flight attendant, a woman with an overflowing heart dedicated to traveling the world and celebrating the humanity she sees within it.

Now you have the best of those poems nestled into one book.

As with the finest of cashmere, Mary spins her words simply and elegantly into beautiful poems that uplift, surprise, delight and open your heart.

Keep this book nearby as your companion to open frequently. Her words create emotion and feeling and set the stage for what is most important, inspiring and transformative:

Remembering that life's greatest gift is to love and be loved.

DEBBIE PHILLIPS
Martha's Vineyard, MA
June 25, 2020

INTRODUCTION

My wish is to inspire people to feel divine love when reading my poems.

I hope to inspire people to have a personal connection to divine love.

The deep wisdom of your higher self is found in your heart where you will find peace and comfort.

I invite you to find a sacred space to enjoy my heart opening poetry.

QUOTES

RUMI, a 13th Century Persian Poet

"In your light I learn how to love. In your beauty, how to make poems. You dance inside my chest where no-one sees you, but sometimes I do, and that sight becomes this art."

"I looked in temples, churches, and mosques. But I found the Divine within my heart."

"Listen to presences inside poems, let them take you where they will. Follow those private hints, and never leave the premises."

"Why are you knocking at every other door? Go, knock at the door of your own heart."

AGAPI STASSINOPOULOS, from her book *"Unbinding the Heart"*

"We are all holding on to something that separates us from our heart. But if we can go inside and find that something—and it takes courage to reveal it to ourselves, recognize it, and heal it—we may discover that our hearts are always accessible. It takes a shift in awareness and a willingness to let go. If we can let go of whatever holds us back from loving ourselves just the way we are—all of our faults, all those thoughts that undermine us, all those feelings of not being good enough—the gate will open all by itself."

ROB BERKLEY

"Life is precious, don't waste a drop."

THE CALLING

Nestle into the sweetness of your heart.

Your heart is where love resides.

In the depth of your heart lives the wisdom of the
ages.

Your truth,

your passion,

your likes and dislikes.

Do not ignore its message.

Your life will become a masterpiece when you
quietly tune into its calling.

Nestle into the sweetness of your heart.

THE GOLDEN KEY

Let go, let God whisper precious golden words
    into your heart.
Let the words wash over you.
Come and seek the golden key to open the door to
    your ancient heart.
Old patterns must dissolve.
You are a golden light that shines its peaceful
    radiance.
Come to the water's edge and seek the golden
    nugget you are seeking.
Release all your emotions into the air.
Let them fly away into the ether of time.
Put your hands up to the sky and surrender to
    the loving arms of love.
Let go, let God whisper precious golden words
    into your heart.

THE ETERNAL GARDEN OF LOVE

The eternal garden of love springs forth from
your heart.

Remember to clean out old growth and water
your infinite heart.

Your well of ancient wisdom can be tapped
into when you look into your heart's deep
reservoir.

Your boundless wisdom is waiting for you to
arrive and seek its timeless counsel.

The eternal garden of love springs forth from
your heart.

OUR HEARTS BEAT LIKE THE SOUND
OF A DRUM

Our hearts beat like the sound of a drum.

Pause and recognize its wondrous ways.

Put your hand on your heart.

Can you feel its warm glowing energy?

O cherished one, this is your connection to divine
love.

During the day remember to connect to deep love
to remind yourself how beautiful you are.

Our hearts beat like the sound of a drum.

WE CAN CONNECT TO THE DIVINE SPIRIT IN OUR HEART

We can connect to the divine spirit in our heart.
Do not let your tribal ancestors tell you of deceit
    that lies in your heart.
"Be gone", I said of thee.
We are here to express our holy gifts in our short
    lifespan on Mother Earth.
We can connect to the divine spirit in our heart.

THE FERTILE SOIL OF YOUR THIRSTY HEART

Settle down into the fertile soul of your thirsty
heart.

Sit still with words of wisdom that rise from your
awakening.

In time, these seeds of wisdom will burst into a
beautiful ray of sunshine.

Your divine splendor will spread to the mountain
tops and settle upon the morning clouds.

Love has no boundaries.

Settle down into the fertile soul of your thirsty
heart.

DO YOU SEE THE SIGNS OF THE SPIRIT?

Follow your spirit-filled heart.
Do you see the signs of the spirit?
The waves crashing, thunder blasting.
Do you see the signs of the spirit?
The billowing clouds are forming into a
symphony of peace.
We know its love language.
We understand its message.
Follow your spirit-filled heart.

LISTEN TO THE WHISPER
LISTEN TO THE WHISPER

Listen to the whisper.

Listen to the whisper.

Can you hear it?

The divine voice is soft and calming.

Walk peacefully, walk calmly and surrender.

Your heart will swell with delight because the
unfolding of your life's path will be clearly lit.

Listen to the whisper.

Listen to the whisper.

CLOSE YOUR EYES AND SLOWLY TUNE INTO YOUR INNER VOICE

Close your eyes and slowly tune into your inner
voice.

What do you hear?

Deep inside yourself are the answers to life's
deepest questions.

Are we kind to ourselves?

Do we love ourselves?

Do we forgive others?

Close your eyes and slowly tune in to your inner
voice.

LET US CONTEMPLATE THE UPS AND DOWNS
OF LIFE

Let us contemplate the ups and downs of life.

Life has its eternal flow,

of course, a very mysterious adventure.

Some roads we have taken have curves, some are
straight, some steep and others lead downhill.

We can ride these paths and stay centered in our
hearts.

Believe in your innate wisdom.

Let us contemplate the ups and downs of life.

GRACE

Lovely is the hand of God,

the graciousness of his provisions.

Let us face our own reality and embrace our
imperfections.

Let us plunge into the well of transformation.

Let the hand of God wash us clean as snow as we
become covered in grace.

Let the cleansing light soak into our souls, fill
our deepest desires for contentment, peace
and joy.

Lovely is the hand of God.

AWAKEN OUR SLUMBERING HEART

Take off the veil that covers all the illusions
    around your heart.
Let your false beliefs be taken away by a mighty
    gust of wind.
Let your voice whisper a sweet melody that
    slowly awakens your slumbering heart.
Your heart will begin to beat a steady river of
    divine love.
Relinquish your past and step into the newness
    of forever—your eternity.
Take off the veil that covers all the illusions
    around your heart.

LET THE FIRE OF TRANSFORMATION SWEEP AWAY YOUR SHADOWS

Let the fire of transformation sweep away your shadows.

Let your life changing ashes be thrown to the wind.

You have a new heart, a new way of looking at life.

You can see the splendor in the ordinary.

Be grateful and have deep compassion.

Your presence has a calming effect to offer the world.

Let the fire of transformation sweep away your shadows.

LET SPIRITUAL WISDOM PENETRATE YOUR HEART

Let spiritual wisdom penetrate your heart.
If your heart is broken, it can be mended.
Do not let shadows stop your brilliance.
Our broken hearts can beat again and become
    extraordinary.
Burst free!
Your sweet soul can take a fresh new breath
like the breath of a newborn baby.
Let spiritual wisdom penetrate your heart.

LET LOVE HOLD YOU IN ITS ETERNAL ARMS

Let love hold you in its eternal arms.

Let love take away all your anxiety.

Love has come to bring you peace and thoughts
of everlasting joy.

Breathe into love and your capacity to love will
increase.

Let love hold you in its eternal arms.

LET OUR HEARTS SURRENDER TO EVERLASTING LOVE

Let our hearts surrender to everlasting love,
a love that transcends human love.
This love is so beautiful that it will carry us
    through this lifetime.
The blessings of divine love are as vast as an
    ocean.
Its waves of love can wash over us and release
    our heartaches.
Let our hearts surrender to everlasting love.

LOVING TEARS

Let love wash your tears away.

Let them slowly drift away down into the river of
    eternity.

Tears will soothe a heartache.

Let us not take for granted the beautiful gift of
    cleansing tears.

Tears are like a beautiful waterfall in a forest that
    flows into a pool of memories.

Let love wash your tears away.

SWING YOUR HEART TOWARDS
THE PATH OF FOREGIVENESS

Swing your heart towards the path of
forgiveness.
Leave all your worries behind.
Lay down your burdens and let them rest upon
Mother Earth.
Burdens are eliminated when you breathe out and
let go.
Your sweetness will appear again.
Your glowing eyes and radiant smile will light up
the room.
Your peaceful presence will lead the way.
Swing your heart towards the path of forgiveness

DEEP WELLS OF DELIGHT
LIE DEEP IN YOUR HEART

Dive deep.

Dive deep.

The river of love flows in your heart.

Dive deep.

Dive deep.

In the vastness of the depths of your heart, you
    will find peace.

Find it.

Cherish it.

Visit it daily.

Transform your life,

your inner being.

Deep wells of delight lie deep in your heart.

ENTER THE POOL OF LOVE

Enter the pool of love,
a quiet, sacred place
where our souls can be renewed.
We lie down and feel the presence of healing
    hands.
The energy is so powerful.
We know we have been touched by an angel of
    love.
Believe, believe, believe.
Enter the pool of love.

DIVINE LOVE SHOWER ME WITH YOUR HEALING LIGHT

Divine love shower me with your healing light.

Embrace me, show me and help me to find my
way.

Let me seek you during the day when the sun is
shining.

Let my face light up when the glow of your truth
engulfs me.

Divine love shower me with your healing light.

DEEP WATERS OF LOVE

Seek divine love from deep in your heart.
Its essence overflows like a beautiful gushing
    waterfall.
It plunges down deep into your soul.
It sustains you when the winds of change are
    upon you.
Just tap into its deep refreshing spring of delight
    and your
heart will swell with a radiant glow.
Now go, be still and know you are an everlasting
    soul.

THE GREAT PAUSE

The great pause.

Such needed rest.

The great pause.

Our hearts can slow down.

The great pause.

We can reflect and make our life anew.

The great pause.

Our values come into view.

The great pause.

We crystallize our future.

The great pause.

Our future is bright with our shining light.

SWEETNESS IS THE KEY TO A HAPPY HEART

Sweetness is the key to a happy heart.
Let your heart begin to renew its candy-like
    taste.
Oh, let all your hurts and pains diminish like a
    chocolate bar melting in your mouth.
Let your delighted heart twinkle into eternity!
Sweetness is the key to a happy heart!

LET THE SUN SHINE UPON YOUR FACE

Let the sun shine upon your face.

Be the fragrant flower in life's garden.

Remember to plant yourself in fertile soil.

Your soil must be watered with love.

Pull out the weeds of life.

Remember we are here to transform our spirit
    and soar with the winds of time.

Let the sun shine upon your face.

LIGHT AS A BIRD WE FLY

Light as a bird we fly.
Let us soar above our earthly cares with grace
and ease.
Let us not be weighed down by our earthly fears.
Let our spirits fly high like a bird in the sky.
Light as a bird we fly.

LET US FLY HIGH HELD
BY THE ARMS OF LOVE

Let us fly high held by the arms of love.

Fly high, soar, surrender and let go.

Be free, be light, be love.

Always true, always light with no resistance –
    only compassion.

Release and fly.

Release and fly.

Release and fly.

Let us fly high held by the arms of love.

EVERLASTING LOVE

Take me away into your loving arms.
Let my heart melt like butter.
I know love when I find it.
The joy it brings is everlasting.
My heart is singing a new song,
a song of joy and peace.
Take me away into your loving arms.

OPEN YOUR HEART
LIKE A BUDDING PINK ROSE

Open your heart like a budding, pink rose.

The petals are soft and velvet—like to touch.

Know that when you open your heart to divine
    love

it enters and brings amazing, heavenly creations.

You are the voice of the divine.

You are the arm of the divine.

Humble your heart and surrender.

Open your heart like a budding, pink rose.

REMEMBER WE CAME
FROM HEAVENLY STARS

Remember we came from heavenly stars.

You are a beautiful ball of light sent down to this
earth to heal your soul.

Remember all your healing is an inside job.

You have come to awaken your spiritual
brilliance.

Your light is burning a brilliant flame.

You are becoming more confident in the wisdom
of your heart.

Remember we came from heavenly stars.

A LIGHT IS SHINING FROM OUR EYES

A light is shining from our eyes.
As we transform our inner being
our eyes glow like a candle's flame.
Our inner peace gets brighter and brighter as we
    follow the inner wisdom of our hearts.
We have been searching for this love and wisdom
    our whole lives.
Finally, we have discovered it resides within us.
A light is shining from our eyes.

LET US WALK OUR EARTHLY JOURNEY WITH PEACEFUL SHOES

Let us walk our earthly journey with peaceful
   shoes.
So, when we walk upon Mother Earth
we will tread lightly and appreciate her beautiful
   gifts:
a rose garden, a meadow of flowers and a
   snowcapped mountain.
Let us walk our earthly journey with peaceful
   shoes.

A SONG OF LOVE AND UNDERSTANDING

Listen carefully to the song you are about to sing,
a song of love and understanding,
a song so deep that the sparrow understands the
    melody.
Nature longs for the reunion of your true essence,
your truth, your deep connection to spirit.
Believe in your heart that you will find the river
    of love.
Be kind to yourself; your presence is all you need.
Connect to the divine spirit.
Listen carefully to the song you are about to sing,
a song of love and understanding.

MY HEART IS OPEN TO NEW POSSIBILITIES

My heart is open to new possibilities,
to a future I have never seen before.
My eyes widened to peer out into the vast fields
    of the unknown.
As I hold a dandelion, I make a wish and blow the
    seeds into the wind,
hoping my intentions will land on fertile ground.
Let my heart be open to new dreams,
so my eyes will glow like the afternoon sun.
My heart is open to new possibilities.

WIDE OPEN PAGES

Wide open pages,
a new story that needs to be written,
a love story between yourself and divine love.
Wide open pages written deep in your heart.
Only you can access this love story.
Wander down the path of love.
A beautiful love story is about to unfold.
Wide open pages.

SOFTEN YOUR HEART
TO THE WINDS OF CHANGE

Soften your heart to the winds of change.

Your steps are divinely guided.

Soften your heart to the winds of change.

Open your heart and listen to the whisper.

A powerful change is upon us.

You are strong and courageous.

Soften your heart to the winds of change.

YOU ARE A LAMP FOR THE LIGHT OF LOVE

You are a lamp for the light of love,
so precious and true.
Your divine dance is whirling like a powerful gust
of wind.
Your heartbeat grows stronger as you dip your
toe into the river of love.
You can feel its current transforming your energy
to an illuminating glow.
You know you have found your way.
You are a lamp for the light of love,
so precious and true.

BREATH GENTLY SWEET ONE

Breathe gently, sweet one.
Your breath is precious and divine.
It connects you to your truth and your voice.
Breathe out the goodness that lies in your heart.
Your heart is your divine essence.
It carries your sweet spirit of goodness and love.
Release its wonderous essence into the world,
 and it will encourage others to do the same.
Breathe gently, sweet one

THE LIGHT OF FOREVER

Breathe into the transcendent light,
the light of forever
where words are formed and manifest into
    reality.
Breathe into the sweetness of your favorite love
    song
so that it penetrates your heart so deeply that the
    words move your heart to love.
Deep in a love song is a reminder that you can
    open your heart for a new beginning.
Breathe into the transcendent light,
the light of forever.

REMEMBER WE CAME FROM LOVE

Remember we came from love.
Let the beauty of love shine upon us.
Let it penetrate deep into our hearts.
Let love continue to bring us peace.
Remember we came from love.
Our heavenly heart is so precious.
Let us surrender to the calling of love
as it transforms and enlightens us
so, we can continue to
shine like a diamond.
Remember we came from love.

GRATITUDE

To my husband, Tom, who is always the first person to hear my poems and tell me if they are beautiful.

To Debbie Phillips whose love and support has encouraged me to discover my own voice and talents and share them with the world.

In loving memory of Rob Berkley who taught me to "take persistent, focused action", which motivated me to write my poetry book.

To Agapi Stassinopoulos whose heartfelt books and support inspired me to follow my heart.

To my good friend, Carrie Saba, whose belief in me inspired me to shine my light in the world.

To all my Women on Fire friends who have supported and encouraged me to stand strong in my own gifts and talents.

To all my friends whose love and support have made me realize my poetry has a message that resonates in hearts.

To my sister, Amy, for her loving support.

To Lucy Giller, at Little Gem Studio, for her beautiful book cover and interior design.

To my poetry consultant, A. Anupama, whose skilled editing I deeply appreciated.

To Andrew Fox for his additional editing.

To authors, Alexandra Franzen and Lindsey Smith, for their guidance and instruction on how to self-publish my poetry collection through their Tiny Book Course.

ABOUT THE AUTHOR

Mary Burnett Brown is a mystical poet, photographer, and an international flight attendant. She lives in The Rocky Mountains in Colorado, surrounded by wildlife, with her husband Tom and two cats.

As a flight attendant for thirty-seven years, Mary has logged countless miles on an airplane. Some of her favorite cities are London, Hong Kong, Amsterdam and Madrid. Through all her travels and time spent with thousands of people from around the world, Mary has come to realize that all people desire peace and happiness.

Mary desires to continue bringing happiness to people through her poetry. Through her travels, meditation, as well as following positive teachers, Mary will find the divine words that speak to people's heart.

Mary Burnett Brown Poet

@marybrownsheartpoetry

www.maryburnettbrown.com

CPSIA information can be obtained
at www.ICGtesting.com
Printed in the USA
LVHW111633151220
674264LV00031B/265

9 781735 544601